A Raga for George Harrison

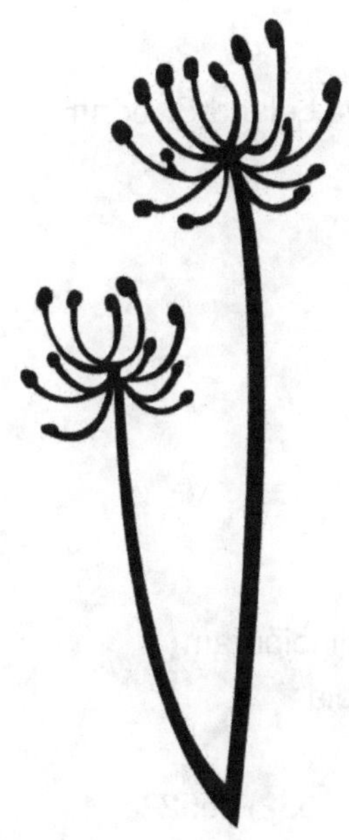

Sharmagne Leland-St. John

Contents

Contingencies

In Azcapotzalco,
I remember mostly
their dark eyes,
their round, brown faces,
Mexican bowl haircuts,
and then,
the outstretched, dirty palms
on the end of spindly arms,
tiny hands,
with ragged fingernails.

In Welligama,
on palm-fringed beaches
they encircled us.
Their dry, cracked lips begging
for a two-pence.
"One two piece, one two piece,"
They chanted.
Clad mummy-like in rags,
gray from the mud of streets,
The filth of poverty—
Their smiles engaging.

I have seen them in Cairo,
near the City of the Dead.
Where the deceased "live" better
than the living.
Hauntingly beautiful children,
maimed, crippled, scarred

by their parents
in order to elicit pity,
hence silver and copper coins,
from the rich American tourists.

In Lima, in front of the Cathedral
which held the catafalques
and Pizarro's tomb,
a gypsy woman tried to hand me
a baby, pleading,
"Un regalo, un regalo"
As I reached out for "her gift"
you held me back.
"Don't take it," you hissed.
"She'll run away."
I stood there,
in the shadow
of the basilica
in sombre half-light,
in the cobbled streets
of this foreign city—
my barren heart,
my fallow womb
needing the baby,

But you pulled me away.

La Kalima

Like swallows they return each year
their vermilion scarves stirring
in the relentless,
oppressive, scalding Sciroccos.

They come amber-scented
from Tunisia,
the hems of their lilac kaftans
fluttering in Zephyr's
white-hot breath.

They come from Kashmir
with mehndi stained hands and feet,
physical graffiti,
their silk saris whispering raginis
pitched to sultry winds.

They come from Cairo
their kohl eyes
searching the bazaar
for the delicate spider web lace,
the rondels woven by
needle-pricked fingers.

They come from Andalusia
with jessamine and geranium
pinned into the lustrous ripples
of their burnished ebony hair.

They come and they go
to return each year like swallows.

Lilipoh Winter 2020

A Raga for George

for George Harrison
1943 - 2001

PBS Reno
just played
the Concert for George.
Stepping outdoors,
the moon is bright,
an incandescent ball,
glowing.

Weatherman said
"Partly cloudy."
A sprinkle of stars twinkle
in the Northern sky.
The night is brisk;
the crunch of ice beneath my feet,
recalls a bundled-up childhood
of sledding
down snow white hillocks
in a small Eastern town,
so far away in time and memory.
A gentle wind is blowing,

Though most of the land
is now brown earth,
not snow,
It is the sounds one remembers

long after the visuals are gone.
Or going.

To see the night sky
in all its glory,
and to hear George Harrison's music
lilt across this high desert plain
is breathtaking.
And to know glaciers were right here
long ago.
This was the very edge of them,
for awhile.
A strong connection is growing.

Sitar strings sing
and reverberate
in this desert night,
his music still flowing.

Claudia's Song

Many a young rose dies on the vine
The brier and the wild rose intertwine
Snail trails glisten on the garden walk
The tales they would tell if the flowers could talk
Yesterday a leaf fell down
Gold and crimson to the ground
Now the wind has swept it far away
The stillness is like a færie glade
The green moss grows in the heart of the shade
The blue-jay shrieks, a whippoorwill calls
Ivy is creeping up the cold stone walls
Tulips lay napping in their rich dark beds
The daisies are nodding their scented heads
The sundial counts the hours that have passed
While you lay sleeping
The trees are tall the breezes fast
Some say the summer sun won't last
Many a young rose dies on the vine
The brier and the wild rose intertwine
While nestled in amongst the flowers
The sundial counts the hours

For Claudia Jennings (Mary Eileen "Mimi" Chesterton)
1949-1979

Pearl's Song

They came to mourn
They came to cry
They came to wonder
How someone so young
Could ever die

She had fame and fortune in her youth
The songs she sang were songs of truth

The moon it waned, the moon it waxed
Her train was slippin' down the tracks
The sky was dark the clouds were pale
When she rode out on a midnight rail

I remember her in the studio that night
Restless, and her voice was tight
All in a knot
Yet when she said goodbye who would have thought
She'd never see the morning light
But the sky was dark and the clouds were pale
And she rode out on the midnight rail

They came to mourn
They came to cry
They came to wonder
How someone like her
Could ever die

Although it's been over 30 years

Since we shed our loving tears
Since that night
When we kissed and said goodbye
Your star has never dimmed
Your ashes were scattered in a gentle wind.
The sky was dark and the clouds were pale
When you rode out on the midnight rail

for Janis Joplin (Pearl)

January 19, 1943 - October 4, 1970

Ariel

in Winthrop
beach behind house
storm behind cloud
beside azalea path
near the grave
of Otto Plath
before cloud
hid sun
before depression
had begun
before deceit
before letters home
had changed their tone
before despair

on Primrose Hill
no band of angels
could ever heal
nor soothe
nor salve
with balm
or metaphor
for Ariel
she is no more

for Sylvia Plath
1932 – 1963

Rite of Passage
(In memory of Virginia Woolf)

London

born of death
a child dreaming
in this mayhem
of patchwork siblings
all a jumble
as you huddled
in your feather bed
cuddled
in Vanessa's arms
what voices
whispered to you?
what flavour was
the taste of dread

Cornwall

a young girl dreaming
looking over
Porthminster Bay.
Godrevy Lighthouse
emblazoned forever
on your mind
how was your
happiness defined
losses left their mark
shell-shocked survivors

victims
propelled a little further
against the dark
your motifs of emptiness
and absence
haunt us to this day
who will describe
the empty room
you left behind?

East Sussex

what did the voices
whisper to you
on that day?
were you afraid
of growing old?
the March winds
the river Ouse
deep and cold
did not deter you
from the madness
of your task or
the sickness in
your mind

familiar stones
you skipped on waves
along the Cornish coast
now weighed you down
beside a foreign shore
what of the loved ones
left behind?
like you'd been left before

it took three weeks
to find you
your bones were laid to rest
beneath a garden tree

in what language
do the birds sing now
perched upon
the dappled bough?

Love-In

Bearded Buddha,
sufi, hare krishna,
beatnik, former Jew
swathed in white,
semi lotus position
on the ragged edge
of Sheep Meadow.

Awestruck hippies
circle round,
listening, bobble-headed
to the anaphoric repetition
as the bard recites.

In an acid haze
I listen...
watch the roses grow
from the top of your head
hear the wind howl.

The leaves of grass die,
yet are reborn
at your slippered feet.

I am entranced
by your yellow shadow,
your blood red sash.

Above the birdsong
lilts an ocarina
dulcet and shy,
your finger cymbals
like Tibetan tingsha bells
ringing, singing.

On this crisp
Easter Sunday Morning
Nineteen Hundred and Sixty-Seven,
I too fathom
the interconnectedness of the universe.

Central Park
like an anthill,
teeming with tie-dye,
eusocial creatures.

In the middle of
your *Kaddish for Naomi*,
the barefoot boy
with flowers
in his blonde
leonine hair and beard
exclaims,
"Wow man, groovy!"

You shoot him
a withering glance
then your eyes meet mine
and for a split second
I see into your soul.

"Hare Krishna Hare Krishna
Krishna Krishna Hare…Hare,
Hare Rama Hare Rama
Rama Rama Hare…Hare."

You give penumbra
a whole new meaning.

For Allen Ginsberg
1926-1997

Upon Going To Erica's Office On Second Street For the First Time

She said it was between
the tattoo parlour and the psychic,
but did not allude to the fact that Allen Ginsberg
lived there from August 1958 to March of 1961.
Didn't mention that it was across the street
from Klean & Kleaner
and on the same block as Chase Bank.
Did not think to describe the blue fire escapes,
Limpet-like, clinging to
windowed walls.
Or its juxtaposition to
the East Village Lounge
that probably wasn't there
in Ginsberg's day.

Didn't say a word about the sprawling graffiti
sprayed on the red brick wall at #171
Perhaps didn't remember the
yellowed leaves of the honey locust tree
with its brown pods hanging
over cracked cement sidewalks;
nowhere to drop its fertile seed.
Maybe she never looked up to note
the acanthus, the egg and dart,
the Greek key, the lamb's tongue;
buildings crowned
by an ornamental frieze

with their pigeon-soiled stoops,
common walls and iron gates.

Not a word was said
about the mournful elegy he wrote
for his mother in apartment 16
just before he moved.
Or that the new tenants,
when the wind howls
and rain spatters against the pane,
sometimes hear a harmonising
click and clack and ding
of a Smith-Corona,
around midnight,
while his spirit
hammers out a Kaddish for himself.

Lorca

1898 –1936

Across the ochre meadow
He stumbled,
Blindfolded.
Wildflowers dotting
Unfamiliar terrain quivered
In morning's cool breeze.
The same gentle wind
Slightly ruffled his hair.

For a brief moment
Clouds obscured sun.
Then the high-pitched
Click and clink
Of metal upon metal–
Ammunition loaded,
Rifles cocked,
While butterflies danced
An erratic air ballet.

How would he have described
The staccato sound of a firing squad
As it shatters the golden dawn?
Or should one perhaps
Refer instead
To the sudden cessation of birdsong
Then the silken whisper of wings…
Beating

Against a blood-drenched sky;
As seen through
The dead poet's eye?

Matilde

for Pablo Neruda
1904 - 1973

Did she slake your thirst
and fill your poet's heart
with flowery words
to spill across the empty page,
a river of green ink,
flowing?

Did you see the rainbows
in her eyes and pray
she'd never leave you,
as you had left the others?

Did you watch with wonder
when she twined the blossoms
of the bougainvillea
into tangled locks
and feel your soul
was laughing at the moon?

Did you listen for her footsteps
on the spiral stair,
waiting for her return
so you could breathe again?

Did you ever think
someone could love you
so completely?

Eulogy for Hector Pieterson

1964 – 1976

He will not speak in syllables now
He will not utter a sound
in English, Xhosa, or Afrikaans

But he will speak volumes
through his martyrdom
this 13 year old,
this boy,
this child
who took a bloody stand
who took a bullet
from a white man's hand

This young "coloured" boy
not black, mind you, but "coloured"
in a colour-conscious nation
of murderers and enslavers
who would massacre children
for the colour of their skin or
for speaking their mind

This boy who joined his
Soweto classmates
in a peaceful protest
to resist learning a language
no one wanted to teach,
let alone speak

this hated language
of their oppressors
no one wanted to learn
these words that would fall
from this child's pink mouth
like boulders, not like
his native tongue, which fell

like smooth stones
washed by the river
these words.

His sister Antoinette
will never forget
she will always hold
in her memory
in her mind's eye
the sight of him
limp and lifeless
on that fateful day
in the strong
young-man arms
of Mbuyisa Makhubo
weeping as he ran
weeping as he
raced against time
Hector's red blood
staining his coveralls
and his name
running toward the press car
towards the photographers
and journalists
who have made her brother famous

only in death
Mbuyisa Makhubo
who had to go into hiding
forced to flee his homeland
for helping
to try to save this child's life

Hector's voice clear
as he sang the hymn
Nkosi Sikelel' iAfrika
he was one of many
but not the first child
to take a bullet
just the first to die
and then to celebrate
his only and most important
rite of passage

Death

Hector and Hastings Ndlovu
now rest in Avalon
side by side
and their voices echo
hollow
in our ears forever …
Nkosi Sikelel' iAfrika

Anna Mae Pictou~Aquash
1945-1975

anna mae
who will braid your hair
this ancient ritual
now a task of great despair
by an unquiet grave
for this woman warrior
at Wounded Knee
we knelt and prayed
for you were once
a part of this creation

anna mae
who will polish your fingernails
the FBI?
you had no right to die
there was no dignity
in the dastardly way
they set your spirit free
how did you come to harm
and who will take
the turquoise bracelet
from your frozen arm

anna mae
you are
water songs unsung
teardrops in the river
a mother

a sister
a daughter
a loving wife
slaughtered
an activist
a human sacrifice
a slice of Indian life

Anna Mae was killed in mid-December 1975 and her frozen body was found two months later on February 24, 1976 in the north-eastern Badlands of the Pine Ridge reserve. The FBI severed her hands and sent them to Washington, D.C., for identification.

Hey, It Was the Sixties!

Peace marches...
"Hell No, We Won't Go!"
Burning draft cards,
Or library cards
If you didn't have a Selective Service card!
"Suppose They Gave a War and Nobody Came?"
Forging birth certificates
To get our friends across the Canadian border
Thinking an FBI "jacket"
Was double-breasted,
But didn't have a Nehru collar
"Help Stamp Out Ugly Children...
Sterilize President Johnson!"
Capping acid in an apartment
On Corbett Avenue,
In Twin Peaks.
Hash brownies
Hanging out at Tracy's Donuts in the Haight.
Panhandling in the Presidio.
Flower children
Out of control!
The Greta Garbo Home
For Wayward Boys and Girls,
Super Spade with his purple paisley shirt
And his generous smile.
The daisy I painted on his black cheek.
You Are What You Eat.
The Chelsea Hotel,
The Tin Angel,

HAiR.
"Let the Sunshine In!"
Windowpane
Owsley
Harvard Yard,
Performing at the Psychedelic Supermarket,
Fillmore East, and Fillmore West, the Ark
Chiding girls from the stage,
"Don't sleep with him again,
until he agrees to resist the draft."
The Boston Tea Party, Club 47,
Monterrey Pop Festival,
Alcatraz,
Woodstock.
The Kinara Institute
Ravi and George
Ali Akbar and Sadruddin
"Rainy Day Raga"
Ice Bag, Maui Wowie, Elephant Grass.
R and R on Waikiki
Ranny Walrod offered me a lift
In a C-141 aircraft
From Honolulu to L.A.
On his way back from 'Nam,
Any time I wanted,
But Jim Dixon told me
There were body bags in the cargo hold.
So I declined.
You didn't meet me
In front of the Palacio de Belles Artes
In Mexico City,
That long hot summer,

As we had planned when we said goodbye
On Graduation Day...
You were in one of those bags.

For Michael Grimes
1946-1965

Wild Dark Love Song

Her man,
A wild dark love song.
Borne deep within her gypsy soul.
He's gone to live in jagged mountains,
Where salmon jump and sing,
In tarns
High above
The cloud lines
Beyond the silver moon.
In the shadow of the Cader Idris
In misty mountains,
Where meadowlarks are known to wing,
And wild geese fly,
Across the winter sky.
He's gone to live in snow-capped mountains
Where frozen voices echo,
Across the frosty fields,
Across the icy meadow,
Languidly, across the frigid lea,
Then back again.
He's gone to her forever.
This wild dark love song,
Her man

For Richard Sylbert
1928-2002

An Unsung Song To Ron

I'm the one who brought you rainbows
When you had thought I only brought the rain
The one who tried so hard through loving
To gently ease your pain
The one who was afraid to love
But thought she'd take the chance
The one you sought to send away
Without a backward glance
The one who woke up Sunday morning
To see through anguished eyes
That a cherished part of her
Had turned away and died
And the night, which passed so slowly
Had only been in vain
I'm the one who'll try through silence
To win you back again
When you look in Monday's mirror
Will you understand a woman's fears
And when you see the rain next time
Will it remind you of my tears?
I'm the one who tried so hard
To gently ease your pain
The one who brought the sunshine
And chased away the rain
The one who tried so hard through loving
To gently ease your pain
The one who'll try through silence
To win your love again.

Written for Ron Talsky
1936-1996
Inflight to New Zealand

Things I Would Have Given To My Mother Had She Asked:

A piece of my liberal mind.
5 more minutes of my time,
the night she called at 3 am
from Halls Lake, WA to L.A.,
drunk, slobbering down the phone,
a repetitious sobbing,
tongue thick with Canadian whiskey
and a cacophony of "I love you!"

I told her to call back
when she was sober,
so I'd know she meant it,
then put the receiver down
and returned to my lover's arms

I would have given her
the framed watercolour of the pink roses
in the blue and white pitcher
resting on a white Victorian lace doily,
The one I painted for her Christmas gift,
after I got to know her,
and decided I actually liked her.

The painting I knew
she had no worldly need for
on Thanksgiving eve
the night the phone call came

from an incoherent brother
on his birthday.

Did his stunned words not make sense,
or did I just not want to believe
I was hearing him correctly?
Could not fathom that she could be gone.
just when I had come to cherish her.

I would give her:
My father's love
if it were mine to give.
My brother's honesty
if there were such a thing.
My sister's nonjudgmental side
If she had one.

Grandfather's pinky ring
in my safekeeping.

The black velvet scarf
with the French silk-ribbon embroidery,
tiny roses with cultured pearls
on their stems,
I sewed stitch for stitch
with deft and slender hand.

My treasured first edition copy
of *Green Mansions*.
A favourite from her own youth
during the war years
when she herself
was a young girl growing.

A senior at Hollywood High
winning Chamber of Commerce awards
for her own fanciful writing.

The gaudy flowered dress
she admired
bought at The Pleasure Dome
on the Sunset Strip
when I was a Hippie,
a motherless child,
reinventing my ownself
to erase her DNA
from my cells, my bones, my ovum,
and from the strands of
bleached blonde hair
with baby's breath intertwined

I would give her 24 hours of my own life
just to tell her the things
that have gone unsaid.

For Rosebud
1922-1998

Time Slowed

time slowed
and asked me
to remember
childhood
dreams
and fantasies

time slowed
and asked me
to remember
dew-kissed
mornings
the drone
of honey bees
raw scraped knees

drawing
on the sidewalk
with sticks of
coloured chalk
hopscotch
my skate key
for a lagger

time slowed
and asked me
to remember
my sister's
blue-black braids
coiling asp-like

upon the white
embroidered
pillowslips
the streetcar trips
to the penny
candy store
for liquorice pipes
and red wax lips

time slowed
and asked me
to remember
that last frosty
Christmas morning
standing
a thin small child
with stocking feet
in a flannel night gown
on the radiator grate
trying to keep warm
in a house gone cold

time slowed
and asked me
to remember
the hush
that fell
upon the room
the day you died
time slowed
and asked me
to remember
the objects
on your dresser

the bowl
of oatmeal
shaving soap
the brush
tortoise shell glasses
the mirror
that cast
no image now
the comb
your silver
money clip
a cup

time slowed
and asked me
to remember
your leather chair
your gold watch chain
your patchwork quilt
the guilt I felt
the Sunday comics
you read aloud
the pattern on the carpet
your pomade scent
time slowed
and asked me
to remember
the things
my adult memory
had forgot
when time slowed

for Lake Reynolds
1888-1952

Tiny Warrior

You never saw the spring my love
Or the red tailed hawk circling high above
On feathered wings my love
You only knew the snow
You never saw the prairie grasses bend and blow
And undulate like the shimmering indigo sea
You never saw me
Your eyes were closed so tight
They say you put up quite a fight
Somehow your life was over before it had begun and
Gently did I touch and kiss your tiny-fingered hand
Born too soon
You never saw the silver moon
Or the light of a summer's day
Last night I dreamt a gathering of eagles
Had come
To spirit you away
Born too soon
Your tender heart
Could not beat
To the pulsing rhythm
Of life's taut drum

Nikolai 1982-1983

Unconditional Love

I was thinking of your mother today
the first woman you ever loved
the one all others must measure up to
the first sound you ever heard
the beating of her heart
as she nourished you
and dreamt of you
before your birth
cradled there
in the warmth
of her body
which now
has turned
to silver
ashes
in your
hand

I Said Coffee

I said coffee
I didn't say,
"would you
like to cup
my warm
soft breasts
in your
un-calloused,
long,
tapered,
ringless fingered
hands?"

I said coffee
I didn't say,
"would you
like to
run your tongue
along my neck
just below
my left earlobe?"

I said coffee
I didn't say,
"would you
like to
hold me
in your arms
and feel my heart

skip beats
as you press your
hard lean body
up against mine
until I melt
into you
with desire?"

I said coffee
as we stood there
in the jasmine
scented night
my car door
like some modern day
bundling board
separating us,
protecting us
from ourselves
and lust

I said,
"would you
like to go for
a cup of coffee?"
I didn't say,
"would you
like to brush
your lips
across mine
as you move
silently
to bury your face
in my long, silky,
raven-black hair?"

But you said,
"I can't
I'm married
I can't trust myself
to be alone
with you."
so I looked you
dead in the eye
and repeated
"I said coffee"

Pushcart Prize Nominee 2007

Things I'll do now that he's gone

I'll go to Tuscany alone
and flirt with dark eyed men
I'll l buy a zither
and join a gypsy band

I'll paint my toenails fire engine red

I'll learn to write Sanskrit
and leave messages
scrawled in indelible ink
on bathroom walls
in cities with names
 beginning with the letter "Q"

I'll stay in on Thursdays
and cry myself to sleep
on Friday nights

I'll learn to tango
and propagate red roses
with 12 inch stems
devoid of thorns

I'll make wishes on stars
and believe they'll come true

I'll subscribe to Ladies Home Journal

I'll have an affair with Bob Dylan
I'll lose 10 more pounds
and become famous for something truly inane

It could happen you know

There Were Dry Red Days

There were dry red days.
Devoid of clouds.
Devoid of breeze.
Sound bruised
My burning bones.
Dirt cracked my hands
And caked my cheeks
No buds on limbs of trees
No birds on branches
No hope of rain
Scrawny chickens
Kicked up dust
Scratching for food
That wasn't there.
In the stifling stillness
Of the scorched night
We dreamt
Of cool oases
Tropical isles
Emerald bays
Not these dry red days

Daughter

My arms empty,
I would bring you mallow
and apricot blossoms,
if I knew you would not cry
for the wilted-ness of them,
two days hence.

I would bring you
bushel baskets
brimming with love,
if I thought
you would not crave it
from another six years,
already past.

I would bring you
pots of kohl
and pomegranates,
towers of silk and
lumps of myrrh.

Instead I give you
my widow's pension
for your wedding
knowing
it will never be enough.

Nasturtiums

I am thinking poetry...
The phones for once are quiet...
and there are long shadows
inside my room.
At an open window
curtains quiver.
On the hillside.
nasturtiums bloom.

Through sense memory,
or euphoric recall,
I am reminded
of their peppery taste.
Nasturtiums,
also known as "Indian cress,"
cousins to the radish,
fill my wooden bowl
with their asymmetrical
celadon leaves.

Scattered on top,
a gay profusion of flowers,
mostly orange, but some bright yellow,
or the muted colour of Devonshire cream,
others in total contrast,
a velvety, dark, burgundy hue,
tantalise, tease
with their piquant promise.

I used to always cook with flowers
when my life was simpler
and my thumb greener.
Squash blossoms dipped
in a rich cornmeal batter were a staple
at my dinner table.

On lazy, sun-drenched mornings, in Mellery,
roses, boiled with sugar cane,
and reduced to a thick, sweet, ruby-red syrup,
was dripped, from Georgian silver, onto
Belgian waffles.
Rose petal coolers were sipped in summer
beneath the majestic magnolia trees,
as bees hummed their drone-like litany.

The tiny blue flowers
of the rosemary,
the pink and purple blossoms
of the sage and thyme
dotted the bottom
of a large, brown, glazed Mexican bowl,
as we drizzled fruity,
hot, virgin olive oil
from a copper saucepan
over them,
then added more chopped herbs
to steep,
Sending up an aromatic prayer
to the kitchen gods

Then we poured this scented oil
into another bowl
overflowing with cooked pasta shells.
Once anointed,
we carried them,
ceremoniously, through
the catacomb of alabaster,
white, sun-bleached rooms
out to the verandah,
to our waiting guests,
who, with forks raised,
and starched white linen napkins tucked
into blue collars,
or rib-necked sweaters,
awaited this magnificent feast.
The ultimate gift
from Mother Earth

Oh Life

Oh life
Where have you taken me?
'Twas once I was your fair-haired child
Now it seems I'm out of style
Oh life be gentle yet
There are things I can't forget
Like autumn love without regret
When autumn turned to winter
Mottled leaves in circles twirl
Inside the spirits of the girl
Whose arms were once around you
Love where have you gone
Just when I thought I'd found you
Snowflakes dance like feathers round my head
I cannot dream my dreams
In an empty bed
Life is for lovers
That's what you said
Then placed your soul inside me
But now that winter's taken you from sleep
It seems there's nothing left to keep
You here beside me

Poetry of Lies

You filled my childhood
With your poetry of lies
But did not let me hear
Your soft good-byes
I was a ragamuffin, a changeling
A gypsy orphan child
Sweet and shy running wild
The wind and sun they were my song
I did not stay a child for long
My cheeks were roses plucked from stem
My eyes vast pools or dark green gems
I did not stay a child for long
I miss the days you gave me
I can count them one by one
Yet in the web of childhood
I do not regret the things that we have done
You showed me how to brave the world
And not be hurt by sticks and stones
That other people hurled
You taught me lessons
I learned them well
Now I live my life inside a shell
Crack the egg the chicken dies
You filled my childhood
With your poetry of lies
And now there's no one near to hear
The woman in me cry

Seascape

Sea I love the way you tremble
Like my lady lost inside my arms
Lying spent and sighing
Sometimes she thinks
She might be dying
Like a moth who's caught
Between the lampshade and the flame
Hold me tight she whispers
Like the wind that wraps itself around
The tall pine tree
I cling I cannot let her slip away
She is my love
She is who tells me what I am
I am the waiting shining sun
I am the moon whose light
Will help to fill the weary night
With rays of yellow gold
Just like the dawn of yesterday
Sea I love the way you tremble
Your waves will pound and crash upon the sand
Her tangled auburn hair strand for strand
Will mingle with the crystal tears
Your emerald ocean sheds
My lady's laughing sighing
Like a seagull flying
High above your breakers
Tumbling towards the land
She takes my hand and whispers
"Don't let go. I love you so"

Sea I love the way you tremble
Like my lady lost inside my arms
Lying spent and sighing
So like a dying Queen
Between
The crumpled sheets

Cat's Cradle

Drenched starlings perch
on a cat's cradle
of telephone wires
strung against pewter skies,
crisscrossing
blackened chimneys.

Oxidation takes its toll.

Rain-slicked
slate rooftops
mirror clouds
dark with winter's
melancholy.
The whisper of wind
no longer comforts.
Alone I sit
on the window seat,
cold and numb.
I have tears,
hold me.

Bamboo

shadows
in greyscale
dance across
the whitewashed
bedroom wall
leafy patterns sway
recalling memories
of our paper house
near Kyoto
where bamboo stalks
were silhouetted
outside thin shoji
screens
tall and straight,
in the strongest wind
unbending
they survived better
than our flimsy,
fragile house,
now nothing more than
a childhood memory
while the bamboo
became
a magnificent
grove
a forest
of dancing leaves

in the distance
wind chimes tinkle

On the Riverboat That Day

I remember you
so clearly
on the riverboat
that day
with the sun
behind your fair hair
like a halo

we slipped past
the water falls
as droplets of spray
enhanced the air
then danced
on the red lacquered
posts and rails
reflecting rainbows
in your blue eyes
and wetting the green vinyl seat
beside us

You wore a delicate smile
for the camera
or perhaps
from the memory
of the last night
we spent together
a tapestry
of arms and legs

woven together
between the tangled sheets
the bamboo fields
singing in the night breeze
accompanied by the whisper
of palm fronds swaying
playing a summer symphony

When "you" and "me" was still "we"

Now we have gone
our separate ways
you to your ranch in the high desert
surrounded by purple mountains
and foreign night sounds
coyotes and buzzards,
insects
clicking in the dark

and I back to the canyons
I know so well
the hum of traffic
reminiscent of ocean waves
pounding against a distant shore
crickets chirp in harmony
bird song at dawn
as sunlight filters
through the sentinel of trees
I am reminded
of your halo hair
and the smile
you wore

on the river boat
that day
as we drifted
so far apart

Waimea Falls,
Oahu, Hawai'i

All He's Left Me

All he's left me
Are moonbeams in a jar
A box of dusty records
A busted old guitar
Yesterday's just a book of photographs
A calendar on the wall
The songs we used to sing
Memories one and all

Lord I'm gettin' older
A little wiser too
The spirits in my closet
Will help to get me through
Today's a passing moment
Tomorrow's far away
But Baby's silver tears
Are heavy dues to pay

Footsteps on the pavement
Reflections in a stream
His letters tied in bundles
Might be just a dream
Standing in the window
Gazing at the sky
I'd give anything you wanted
Just to see him passing by

I know how it is to be lonely
How does it feel to be free

Baby loved the highway
More than he loved me

Fleur d'Eau
Switzerland 1974
For Richard Sylbert

I Sing You the Morning

my love,
I sing you the morning
as sunlight drenches
the Tokyo sky
and small brown wrens
gather to fly
while I,
in a blue silken kimono
with chrysanthemum sash,
gaze through my window
at a porcelain sky
the colour of ash

in my mind's eye
I picture you
oceans away
and thus
erotically
I begin my day
as I evoke
the memory
of the thrust
of your hips
yours
is the name
that escapes
the darkness
of my parted lips

Yes, I,
in a blue silken kimono
with chrysanthemum sash,
gaze at a sky
the colour of ash

Promised Land

Lonnie wants his promised land
His 40 acres and a mule
But Uncle Sam says "Boy,
Don't be such a fool
Cause I'll be damned
If I'm gonna give you any land.
You're fortunate just bein' alive.
Now don't-cha give me any more of your jive.
You're lucky to be on welfare
And you know it.
So Son, I'd advise you not to blow it."

They don't call it the Promised Land for nothin'
They promised us land and gave us nothin'

Keoni says his Island was a paradise
Then the Haole came
Hungry for wealth they planted their cane
Now we hang our heads in shame
You made us change our pagan ways
You stole away our rainbow days
When you sold away our native land
And on just one hand
I can count all the gifts you gave to me
You brought us rats and leprosy
Our Island is a tourist trap
And Uncle Sam says "Don't talk back!"

They don't call it the Promised Land for nothin'
They promised us land and gave us nothin'

My cousin Mountain Bluebird's mother
Was Crazy Horse's sister
One of the greatest warriors
History's ever seen
But then the cavalry attacked
They put her mama in a dirt floor shack
With a rickety outhouse way out back
Heya! Uncle Sam
We don't want your trackless land
We don't want this worthless sand
Give us back our Promised Land

They don't call it the Promised Land for nothin'
They promised us land and gave us nothin'

Except a million reasons why

Snug Harbor

She reminded me of Snug Harbor
Perfectly starched white shorts
Thin gold chains from Tiffany
Worn on aristocratic ankles
Below shapely suntanned calves
The exotic, erotic scent of Bain de Soleil
Sailboats dotting a ginger horizon
Adirondack chairs with chintz cushions
Displaying huge floral prints
And banana leaves.

She reminded me of Nancy Drew
And Ned Nickerson in his white linen trousers
And Panama hat
Arrow shirt sleeves rolled up
Lobster bakes at eventide
And campfires 'til midnight
Slow dancing in the headlights
Of a baby-blue convertible roadster
Then snuggling in the back
Under a plaid lap robe
Stolen kisses

Strawberries and champagne,
Cucumber sandwiches at the regatta
Country clubs and trips abroad
Belgian chocolate
Cut flowers in a cut-crystal vase
In the foyer

Radcliffe or Wellesley in the fall
Heirloom diamond engagement rings
From a fourth generation
Harvard undergraduate law student
Weekends with his family in the Hamptons
Tennis

She said I reminded her of Coney Island.

Windy City 2004

the windy city has lost its breath
and soul without you here
streets we used to wander
now empty and alone
memories etched in every paving stone

there was the night you had them
set off extra fireworks from Navy Pier
the street names I had come to know so well
now empty and alone
memories etched in every single stone

our old stomping grounds
Michigan, Huron, Erie, Superior
have all lost their magic spell
now empty and alone
memories etched in every brick and stone

the art galleries echo
but it's your voice I long to hear
explaining all the paintings and sculptures
now empty and alone
memories etched on canvas carved in stone

the windy city has lost its breath
and soul without you here
streets we used to wander
now empty and alone
your memory etched in the marrow of my bone

Rose

You traded us for glaciers,
Snowcapped mountains,
Pine forests,
Where icy rivers run.
You traded us for a man
Who would provide a home
For you and your infant son.

Did we haunt your dreams?
2 little girls,
Huddled together,
In the back of a black and white
1949 Kaiser
Police car
Parked at the curb
While you and Dad
Had it out
One last time.

You traded us
For your own father's freedom
To come and go
Unhindered
Across the borders
From Northern Ontario,
To the Gulf of Mexico
You traded us so you could go home
To the lakes and creeks
Where you, with freckled cheeks,

As a barefoot child used to roam.
Where you and the old aunties and cousins
Would go "huckleberrying"
Under the summer Wenatchee sun.

Did you ever dream of us?
2 little girls
Living like Madeline
Under the scrutiny
Of a strait-backed mother superior
And a passel of cruel, pokerfaced nuns?
Did you dream of us
Being locked away in chilly closets,
For weeping at night,
Because we missed you dearly?

Or were we out of sight,
Out of mind?
Were you merely grasping
For any happiness you could find?

Now I am a woman
With children of my own
And I spend my time in your glacial,
Snow-capped Wonderland,
With my Indian cousins,
My Canadian cousins,
Cooking and chopping wood,
Or beading, while they sit reading
In front of a roaring winter fire;
Dreaming of spring
And fair weather
So we can visit your grave

Where you lay sleeping,
Cuddling the memory
Of your infant son.

Ticonderoga Wind

Quietly she listened
With a subtle Mona Lisa smile
As he ever so softly whispered
"I finally figured out your style."
"Oh what is it?" she ventured
Her voice now growing thin
The lacy curtains barely stirred
And the smile became a Cheshire grin
In the passive Ticonderoga wind
Then with the lightest of eagle feathers
You could have knocked her dead
"You use a lot of adjectives,"
He matter-of-factly said
As he lay there, Pasha-like,
Upon her pillowed bed
Is that good or bad she wondered?
Her soul and body bared
As she anxiously and deeply pondered
The information that he shared
And as she leaned back to listen to the raucous blue jays sing
She was eminently aware of one important thing
Without a myriad of adjectives and verbs
She'd never reach the required one hundred and fifty words
Then she provocatively turned toward him with gentle nips
And licked the words right off his tender, smiling lips

Haiku Rules?

Someone
Foolishly decreed
And then some other one
Complacently agreed
With a gesture oh so grand
And a sweep of
His dismissive hand
The word *"cicada"*
Should be
Forever banned
From modern Haiku
And poetry.

Sirs, I ever so strongly
Disagree with you.
3 & 4 syllable words
Like *"cicada"*
And *"stacatto"*
And *"chrysanthemum"*
Should be sprinkled
Liberally
Like wildflower seeds
Wherever and whenever
The poets please!

The Mystery of You

When the first snows came
I stacked more pine logs onto the hearth,
Extra down comforters on the beds,
And I slept in the crook of your arm.
The warmth of you radiating,
Eradicating the icy breath of winter,
My lips searching for your mouth,
Your tender kisses.

In the cold mornings,
No bird song,
They'd all flown south
Their silence echoing
In the frigid wind.
The whiteness like a shroud
Encompassing the pasture.

With the world still asleep,
I tried to decipher
The mystery of you
Etched in your eyes.
We shared intimate moments
Beneath flannel sheets,
Posing questions
That had no answers.
We no longer speak of the past,

Instead
We leave it where it belongs,

And our hearts swell
With feelings
We cannot comprehend.
We can only
Enjoy
The economy of lines
You trace with fingertips,
Picasso-like on my
Breasts, round belly,
And thighs.

The Ring

she was
the lullaby of my womb
and now I photograph her
at the jeweler's
trying on engagement rings
in her cream-coloured
cotton sundress
her hair still wet
from a hasty shower
sitting there
in the same chair
where I sat
not so very long ago,
it seems,
selecting my own wedding ring
she still looks the child
playing dress up,
so I glance beneath
the diamond showcase
to see if her feet
are encased in mommy's
oversized, high-heeled shoes
and I wonder
which one will she choose?

but it's the ebb and flow,
the come and go of things,
that puzzles me the most.

for Daisy Sylbert and David Torres

Grandchild

She feels no urge to have a baby—
that tug and pull which kept me distracted for years,
brought tears when I saw other mothers with their offspring,
their progeny, being pushed in prams,
or strollers through green parks
and flowered gardens in foreign cities.
Pushed by young nannies on wooden plank swings.
She feels no reason to pack trunks full
with baby dresses, bonnets and bibs
to be tucked away in the dark recesses
of the half-basement beneath
her California bungalow,
awaiting that blessed day
when she can play dress-up with that tiny creature,
an actual baby instead of a cloth and plastic doll,
a flesh and blood baby which is a part of her—a part of him,
that man who makes her heart sing like no other could.
She has not felt (the way I did) a child gathering itself to be born;
cannot picture herself with a daughter at her breast
as yellow sunlight slants its way into the darkened room.
Has no wish to feel its gentle sleeping breath upon her own skin
Does not long to hear the fractured words,
skipped syllables, the lisp of phrases…
the name that is her own
from the soft lips of a child
which bears my DNA.
Has no urge to give birth to my grandchild
who will also be a part of him
who made me sing as no other could.

Wedding

We whisper in romantic tongues.
Every word is sacred
Music lingers to tantalise
Forever we celebrate eternity

And the rhythm of man and woman
Together in passionate embrace
Twin breaths of desire

Wild morning winds blow and die away
Like magnificent vivid dreams.
Our voices echo
Silence

Long Time Gone

I want the house to smell like
Canadian bacon again
On foggy Sunday mornings,
While I stay in bed
Working the New York Times
Crossword puzzle
In brown ink,
With your precious
Mont Blanc fountain pen.

I want to go to Musso & Frank's
On a Thursday night
For fried oysters
And hear your lyric tale unfold—
Your stories of Old Hollywood
Back in the Day!

I want to go fly fishing with someone
Who knows what he's doing and is good,
Someone who'll help me with my leaders
And un-snag my windblown flies
When the rocks claim them,
And twigs refuse to let go,

Someone who won't run upstream
And abandon me
At the first sign
Of an Atlantic salmon
Slicing his way through

The icy waters
Of the Northern Tyne.
I want to lie on the white linen,
Down-filled sofa
In our deco living room
In the old Spanish duplex on Croft,
With my head in your lap
Listening to *A Prairie Home Companion*
On the radio
On a Saturday night,
And later in bed, hear you say,
"They don't call it Saturday night for nuthin!"
Then through sleepy, satisfied eyes
Watch your slow grin spread.

I miss London too,
Mr Chow
On a Friday night,
Chelsea,
And the Chinese vases
With single stalks
Of freesia and paper-white narcissus
You bought from the street vendors
And brought home each afternoon
As a love offering
To our cosy little cottage
In Aubrey Walk,

The trips to SoHo
On the Tube,
The Indian restaurants,
The Constable Room
At the V & A,

Tramps,
Farlow's and Hardy's,
Taramasalata,
Chilled Polish vodka,
The Tate,
Coming home together
The night too dark for dreaming,
Sleeping like spoons
Beneath an antique patchwork quilt
I found in a dusty curio shop
On Portobello Road.

I miss the unequalled luxury
Of being in love once again.

Apple Blossoms

apple blossoms
pink and pale
tender blossoms
sheer and frail
on the wind they
float and sail
snowy blossoms
bee's delight
perfumed flowers
scent the night
morning hours
wrens take flight
dainty flowers
lovely sight

Machu Picchu

Montezuma's daughter
had gold strewn at her feet

Men offered you the Koh-i-Noor...

In wistful embrace
you declined the Eiffel Tower,
the pyramids at Sakkara,
an island in the ancient seas
off Madagascar,
the palace at Cooch-Behar,
but you accepted me.

She Wore a Gown of Shadows

She wore a gown of shadows
With dewdrops in her hair
A crescent moon tiara
Stars could nestle there

And twinkle just like diamonds
Reflected in her eyes
The whistling wind, a ghost song
Laced within her sighs

If you heard her laughing
It chilled you to the bone
It wasn't quite a tinkle
Nor was it a dulcet tone

More like breaking glass, I'd say
From her pale and glossy lips
Or like a raging storm
That drowned a thousand ships

Her feet didnae touch the ground
She floated on the air
She wore a gown of shadows
With dewdrops in her hair

Cairn

Carefully she piles the stones
to mark the mountain's summit.
Stacks flat rock on boulder,
round precariously perched
on oval, elliptical on slab.
Teetering testimony
that she has passed through
this stony, barren terrain.

Aligned to solstice and equinox
they stand at sunrise and sunset,
where mountains rose from prairie,
where singing rivers run,
where water tumbles over lips of crag,
where Chinook winds whisper
her destiny.
Here it is written in stone.

Loon Lake

Nights were full of summer
and the days bursting
with the buzz of bees.

Honeycombs and honeysuckle
scented the daytime breeze;
while drifting across the lake,
night blooming jasmine
floated on the dew-laden air.

The echo of loons
as they sang
their whistled songs
on a distant shore
are part of a cherished memory.
lingering there

Now the lap of waves lulls me to sleep
to dream of those childhood summers
and the promises we made
but could not keep.

Upon Awakening

I am an arm
of the night
reaching back
into the darkness
for all things
mankind has destroyed
through negligence
or premeditation

I am the language of grief
the voice of splintered silence
the heartbeat that pounds
like a hammer
in the ears of reason
the conscience of the silent witness
the eyes of thought
haemorrhaging salt tears
of feigned sorrow

I am the sinew woven into the rope
of the hanged man
the shadow of a doubt

I am the taste of blood
on the forked tongue
of mine enemy
the silver that greases the palm
I am the last whisper
you'll hear in the dark

Michael

Michael
Your moods intrigue me
Quiet now brooding
I wonder where your thoughts have been
Then at dinner
I see a side of you
That I have never seen
You make us laugh
The things you say
The smile you flash
Makes the evening slip away
Today you're pensive
Your mind is occupied
I cannot read your thoughts
No one can who's tried
Sometimes you're like a puzzle
That's hard to put together
Your moods are always changing
Just like the English weather
Has the sun come out?
No there's rain, but I think
The sun is trying
I thought I heard you laughing
Or was it was just the murmur
Of a winter wind sighing

For Michael Butler
Warfield, England

Wind Song

It's night time in my mind
The jasmine blooms again
Just another soft reminder
Of the man I called my friend

Baby knew I loved him
Knew the daydreams that I had
Hope that he'll forgive me
For treatin' him so bad

There's a wind out on the ocean
There's a sighin' in my heart
Told my baby I loved him
Swore we'd never part

They say the devil takes the women
Always makes them lie
Baby please forgive me
Didn't mean to make you cry

Your friends will put me down
They'll say I was unkind
I had no rhyme nor reason
To leave my man behind

And I know that you'll defend me
You'll say that I was right
Then you'll softly hug my pillow
All through this lonesome night

For Paul Rothchild
Kona, Hawaii 1973

Dusk Is Falling Gently

Dusk is falling gently
Like her silk scarf on the wind
And it's sad to think
I'll never see her again
Yesterday she said "I love you"
But it didn't mean a thing
She's a child of the night
A bird on the wing
I see her running through the meadow
Putting flowers in her hair
She should never have said "I love you"
If her heart wasn't there
I could have loved her too
And never brought her pain
But I don't think
I'll ever see her again
Baby don't take my heart
And play your sad game
If your heart wasn't there
You've got no one to blame

Oh Butterfly
You should have stayed awhile
And let me trace
With hungry lips
The space within your smile
I see the things you left here
A box of paints, your old blue jeans
Now dusk is falling gently while
Night time only holds
Tomorrow's fragile dreams